CLASSIC *Spirals*

Package **Holiday**

David Walke

Contents

The Travel Agent's ——————————————————————— 3
4 parts: Mr Banks, Sid, Dolly, Harry

The Plane ———————————————————————————— 12
4 parts: Sid, Dolly, Stewardess, Captain

The Island —————————————————————————— 28
4 parts: Sid, Dolly, Captain, Kong

Text © David Walke 1980, 2001

The right of David Walke to be identified as author of this work has been asserted by him in accordance with the Copyright, Designs and Patents Act 1988.

All rights reserved. No part of this publication may be reproduced or transmitted in any form or by any means, electronic or mechanical, including photocopy, recording or any information storage and retrieval system, without permission in writing from the publisher or under licence from the Copyright Licensing Agency Limited, of 90 Tottenham Court Road, London W1T 4LP.

Any person who commits any unauthorised act in relation to this publication may be liable to criminal prosecution and civil claims for damages.

First edition published in 1980 by:
Hutchinson Education
Reprinted in 1990 by:
Stanley Thornes (Publishers) Ltd
ISBN 0 7487 0352 7

Second edition published in 2001 by:
Nelson Thornes Ltd
Delta Place
27 Bath Road
CHELTENHAM
GL53 7TH
United Kingdom

01 02 03 04 05 / 10 9 8 7 6 5 4 3 2 1

A catalogue record for this book is available from the British Library

ISBN 0 7487 6431 3

Printed and bound in Great Britain by Martins the Printers

The Travel Agent's

4 parts:
Mr Banks (travel agent), Sid, Dolly, Harry

Dolly	Is this it, Sid? Is this the shop where we can book our holiday?
Sid	Yes, Dolly, this is it. This is the travel agent's. Can't you see? It says 'Banks Travel' over the door.
Dolly	Shall we go in then?
Sid	Well, Mr Banks isn't going to come out into the street. So we'd better go in.
Dolly	I've always wanted to fly away for a holiday.
Sid	I've always wanted you to fly away for a holiday too, Dolly. Then I can go to Blackpool on my own.
Dolly	Not Blackpool again, Sid. We go to Blackpool every year. I want to go somewhere new.
Mr Banks	Good morning. What can I do for you?
Dolly	We want to go on holiday.
Mr Banks	Well, you've come to the right place.

3

Sid	I don't want a holiday here in a shop.
Dolly	Don't be stupid, Sid. You see, Mr Banks, we want to fly to the sun. We want to see the blue sky, warm sea, golden sand.
Mr Banks	How about the West Indies?
Sid	Is it near Blackpool?
Mr Banks	No, it's near America. Can you swim?
Sid	Swim all the way to America?
Mr Banks	No. I mean can you swim, because the hotel is near the sea. It's good for swimming.
Dolly	How much will it cost to go there?
Mr Banks	£1000.
Sid	£1000? Just for a holiday! I'm not paying that much!
Mr Banks	How about £500?
Sid	Look, all we want to do is see the sun. We don't want to buy it!
Mr Banks	Well, how much have you got then?
Dolly	We've got £45.
Mr Banks	Just £45?

Sid	Take it or leave it.
Mr Banks	Well, I think I can find something. Let's see what I've got.
Dolly	Here, Sid, look out of the window. There's a funny little man standing out there in the rain.
Sid	Stop looking at him, Dolly. If he wants to stand out in the wet with a stocking over his head, that's up to him.
Dolly	Oh Sid, he's coming in here.
Harry	Get them up! This is a stick-up!
Mr Banks	Pardon?
Harry	I said reach for the sky! This is a stick-up!
Mr Banks	You'll have to wait your turn. I'm talking to these two. Now, what about a horse and caravan down the M1?
Harry	Come on! I haven't got all day! This is a stick-up! I want the money!
Mr Banks	I haven't got any money.
Harry	Come on, you can't pull a trick like that on me. This is a bank. I want the money.

5

Dolly	Oh no, love, this is not a bank.
Harry	Come on, you can't fool me. It says 'Bank' over the door.
Mr Banks	No it doesn't, you twit, that's my name. It says 'Banks Travel'.
Harry	Do they?
Mr Banks	No, I don't mean banks travel. This is a travel agent's, and I'm Mr Banks.
Sid	Yes, the bank is next door.
Harry	OK, I'm sorry. My eyes go funny with this stocking over my head. Good-bye.
Mr Banks	Good grief.
Sid	Now then, what about our holiday?
Dolly	Yes, all we want is something hot by the sea.
Mr Banks	How about Brighton gas-works?
Sid	You're talking a lot of hot air. Now come on, find us a holiday.
Dolly	Here, Sid, there's that funny little man outside again.
Mr Banks	Here it is. The holiday of a life-time for £45 – a week at Costa Lotta.
Sid	That's not bad for £45.

Harry	OK, this is a stick-up! Get your hands in the air and give me the money!
Mr Banks	Look, will you get out! The bank is next door!
Harry	Oh no, you can't pull that trick on me! The chap next door just told me that this is the bank.
Mr Banks	What's the matter with you? It was me that told you. This is Banks Travel.
Harry	Oh, not again! I always mess it up. All I want to do is rob a bank.
Mr Banks	I bet you can't even rob a piggy bank.
Harry	I can! I can! Look, this is a sawn-off shot-gun I've got here!
Mr Banks	Yes, but you've sawn the wrong end off!
Harry	I can't help it. It's my eyes.
Dolly	Have you had them checked?
Harry	No, they've always been blue.
Mr Banks	Look, will you put what's left of your gun down and get out of here.
Harry	It's always the same. They all tell me to go away. Nobody loves me. Nobody likes me.

Dolly	Now don't cry, love. What's your name?
Harry	It's Harry. I've had my fill of life. I'm going to end it all. I'm going down to the railway station now to throw myself under a bus.
Sid	You'll have a long wait.
Harry	You see, I can't even kill myself. I was so sick of my life last week that I got 500 aspirins to end it all.
Mr Banks	And what happened?
Harry	Well, after I took the first two I felt a lot better.
Mr Banks	Look, will you cut out the funny stuff. What are we going to do with 'public enemy number one' here?
Harry	I'm too old for robbing banks, you see.
Sid	You're in a bad way, Harry.
Harry	And this leg hurts.
Sid	It must be old age.
Harry	Rubbish. The other leg is just as old and that one doesn't hurt.
Mr Banks	Do you limp all the time?

Harry	No, only when I walk.
Sid	This is slow work. I bet when he robs a bank they give him the money just to get rid of him.
Dolly	I think you need a good holiday, Harry.
Harry	I'll have to try and rob a travel agent's shop then.
Sid	That's a good idea, Harry.
Mr Banks	That is NOT a good idea, Harry!
Dolly	A nice rest and a bit of sun will do you good.
Mr Banks	Why don't you try Devil's Island? They tell me it's nice this time of year.
Sid	Forget Devil's Island. You're a travel agent. You can give him a holiday.
Mr Banks	Oh, all right. Just to get rid of him. What about the south of France? Here's a nice walking holiday in the south of France for two weeks.
Dolly	That sounds nice, Harry.
Harry	Do I fly or go by bus?
Mr Banks	You walk.
Sid	You mean he has to walk to the south of France!?

Mr Banks	Well, it's a walking holiday, isn't it? You've got one week to walk there and one week to walk back.
Harry	I'm not walking to the south of France!
Mr Banks	Why not? It might get rid of your limp.
Sid	It might get rid of his legs!
Dolly	What about Spain? It's nice in Spain.
Mr Banks	OK. Here's a fantastic holiday. Seven days in Costa Lotta. The hotel is only five miles from the beach.
Dolly	That's better.
Harry	Yes. I like the sound of Spain. I might try robbing some Spanish banks.
Mr Banks	OK. Here's your ticket. You fly on Friday. Now limp off.
Harry	Thank you very much. Well, I'll be off. It's been nice meeting you. Now don't move, and don't stick your head out of this door for ten minutes after I've gone or I'll blow it off.
Mr Banks	OK, OK, big guy. We won't follow you. Now just get out.
Dolly	What about our holiday now, Sid?

Sid	Well, I like the sound of Spain as well.
Mr Banks	You're not going to rob me too, are you?
Sid	No. I'd like a holiday in Costa Lotta, not in the nick.
Mr Banks	OK. A week in Costa Lotta for two. That will be £45 each, please.
Dolly	Oh, no! £45 each? But we've only got £45 between us. We need another £45.
Sid	Well, there's only one thing for it. Hang on a minute, Harry. Have you got another stocking?
Harry	Yes, I've got another one in my pocket.
Sid	OK. Give it to me. I want to put it over my head.
Dolly	What are you going to do, Sid?
Sid	Well, if you can't beat them you have to join them. Come on, Harry, I'll show you where the bank is.

The Plane

4 parts: *Sid, Dolly, Stewardess, Captain*

Dolly Come on, Sid. Hurry up or we'll miss the plane.

Sid Oh, shut up, Dolly! This case is heavy! What have you got in it?

Dolly Just a few things to keep me cool in the sun.

Sid Don't tell me, you're taking the freezer.

Dolly No, just some nice summer dresses.

Sid It feels more like a freezer to me!

Stewardess Jet-set holidays calling. Passengers for plane 202 to Costa Lotta come to desk 13.

Dolly Listen, Sid, that's our plane. Where's desk 13?

Sid How do I know? It must be next to desk 12!

Dolly Excuse me, can you tell me where desk 13 is?

Captain	Yes, madam, it's over there, next to desk 12.
Sid	I told you so.
Stewardess	This plane will leave at ten o'clock....
Dolly	Come on, Sid, over here.
Stewardess	Or maybe eleven o'clock....
Sid	I'm coming, I'm coming.
Stewardess	...or, if we get a good wind, even nine o'clock.
Dolly	Hello, is this desk 13?
Stewardess	Yes, madam.
Dolly	We've got seats booked on the plane for Costa Lotta.
Stewardess	Yes, madam, they're over there.
Dolly	What do you mean?
Stewardess	If you've booked a seat, get one from that pile over there.
Sid	You mean from that pile of deck-chairs?
Stewardess	Yes, madam. Get your chair and take it out to the plane with you.
Dolly	Do you mean that this plane has got no seats?

Stewardess	How silly, madam. Yes, of course the plane has got seats. It's just that they're in a big pile over there.
Sid	That's not much good, all the way to Costa Lotta in a plane with deck-chairs.
Stewardess	Well what do you expect for £45 ... Concorde?
Captain	Now then, now then, what's all the fuss about?
Stewardess	It's OK, sir, I'm just telling them about the seats.
Captain	Ah, yes, I think you'll find that the seats with blue and green spots are the best.
Sid	And who are you?
Captain	I'm the captain. I'm flying you to Costa Lotta. Well, I must go and check the plane. Good-bye.
Sid	He said he's the captain. Is that right?
Stewardess	Yes, sir, Captain Trash.
Dolly	He looks a bit funny. There's something about him that's not quite right.
Sid	Yes, I think it's the big boots, the sheep-skin coat, and the goggles.

Stewardess	Well, he likes to fly with the window open.
Captain	Hello again. I've checked the plane and it's still there.
Stewardess	Put your luggage on the scales, please.
Sid	Here's the case.
Stewardess	Put it on the scales, sir.
Captain	Oh, it's too heavy.
Stewardess	You'll have to take something out, or pay more money.
Dolly	Let's get the case open then.
Sid	What did you bring all these dresses for? Why didn't you just put handles on the wardrobe? That would have saved us packing.
Dolly	I just want to look nice, that's all.
Sid	You'll have to change five times a day to wear all this stuff.
Stewardess	Now, put the case on the scales again, please.
Captain	That's better, it's OK now.
Dolly	But what will we do with all the things we've taken out?

Sid	Don't worry, Dolly. I'm not a mug, you know. I'll just stuff these things in my pockets.
Dolly	That's a good idea, Sid!
Stewardess	Just a minute, sir, now you'll have to go on the scales.
Sid	What for?
Captain	You're carrying luggage in your pockets.
Sid	Oh no!
Captain	So if you'll get on to the scales, sir.
Stewardess	Now you're too heavy. You'll have to get rid of something.
Sid	Oh well, that's good, that is! Get rid of something! Shall I cut an arm off or something? Maybe a leg!
Dolly	Now, Sid, don't get upset.
Captain	Yes, sir, don't get upset, it'll be OK. Just sit in the middle of the plane.
Stewardess	And that will be £5 extra.
Sid	What for?
Stewardess	Because you're too heavy.
Captain	You'll have to slim, sir. Get rid of some fat.

Sid	I've just lost £5!
Stewardess	Now, if sir and madam will come this way, we'll get on the plane.
Dolly	Bring the case, Sid, and don't forget the seats.
Sid	You don't need a husband, you need a donkey.
Captain	I'm sorry, sir, we don't let animals on the plane.
Sid	Well, I'm glad we didn't bring the kids.
Stewardess	Here's the plane.
Sid	What, that old heap!?
Captain	Now, now, sir, don't let the rust fool you. She goes like a rocket.
Sid	I hope we don't end up on the moon.
Dolly	What has it got 'US' painted on the side for?
Captain	Umm. . . . It's an old American plane.
Sid	I'll say it's old. I bet it's got an outside loo!
Stewardess	Now, if you'll both follow the other passengers on to the plane, I'll join you in a moment.

Sid	Why? Are we coming apart?
Dolly	Come on, Sid.
Sid	I'm coming, I'm coming.
Dolly	Isn't this good, Sid? I've never flown before.
Sid	You won't be flying now from the look of that plane.
Dolly	Put the seats here, Sid, I want to sit next to the window. Do you think we'll fly above the clouds?
Sid	I don't think we'll even get off the run-way.
Captain	Hello, everybody. Welcome to plane 202 for Costa Lotta. This is Captain Trash who will fly the plane today.
Stewardess	Now, before we take off we've got one little thing to do.
Captain	Yes, just a little game before we go.
Sid	A game?
Stewardess	Yes, sir. Here's the parachute.
Sid	Thank you.
Stewardess	Now, I'll start the music....
Dolly	Oh, how nice.

Captain	And you pass the parachute round. . . .
Stewardess	And when the music stops, if you have the parachute you can keep it.
Sid	What!! Are you telling us there's only one parachute?
Stewardess	Umm. . . yes. Now here goes.
Dolly	Pass it to me, Sid.
Captain	That's it. Keep it going.
Sid	This is crazy.
Stewardess	And the music stops. . . . Now!
Dolly	Oh! Who's got the parachute?
Captain	I have!
Stewardess	Well done, captain.
Sid	I don't like this, I don't like it at all. It's a fix!
Captain	Now then, if you're all ready, we'll get off.
Sid	That's what I'd like to do — get off!
Stewardess	Fasten your seat-belts, please.
Sid	I haven't got a seat-belt on my chair.
Stewardess	What's that round your middle? It's a belt isn't it? Well pull it in a bit.

Dolly	Oh Sid, isn't this good!
Sid	Yes, great. Deck-chairs, one parachute and no seat-belts.
Captain	Hello, captain calling, the engine seems to be OK now.
Dolly	Oh, Sid, we're moving! Just think, we'll soon be in Costa Lotta ... all that sun.
Sid	It's the same sun we have over here. I think we should have gone to Blackpool.
Dolly	It'll be much better at Costa Lotta. Hey, Sid.
Sid	What's the matter?
Dolly	I've just seen a bus.
Sid	Oh, you'll see a lot from up here in the plane. Buses, houses, the lot.
Dolly	No. I mean we've just passed a bus!
Sid	Where?
Dolly	Here. Look, out of the window. Oh, and there's a lorry.
Sid	Let me see. Hey, you're right!
Dolly	And there's a car with a blue flashing lamp. It's following us. It's a police-

	car. What's a police-car doing on the run-way, Sid?
Sid	The police-car isn't on the run-way, Dolly. That fool's got this plane on the road!! Here, you!
Stewardess	Yes, sir?
Sid	You'd better tell the pilot that there's a police-car after us.
Stewardess	Oh, no, not again!
Sid	This is crazy. I've never been in a plane that's been done for speeding.
Captain	Hello, everybody. Captain calling.
Sid	Here it comes.
Captain	Sorry about that. It seems that I turned left at the end of the run-way when I had to turn right.
Sid	Great. He can't even find his way along the run-way. What's he going to be like when we get up into the air!?
Stewardess	Don't worry, as soon as the police have got off the plane, Captain Trash will turn the plane round. Then we'll take off.

Captain	Here we go.
Stewardess	Hold on to your seats.
Sid	If I hold on to mine it'll come to bits.
Captain	Captain calling. We're up, flying at three metres above the ground.
Sid	Three metres?
Captain	And five metres . . . no . . . three metres. . . .
Dolly	I don't like this, Sid.
Captain	. . . no . . . two metres.
Sid	What's he playing at?
Captain	Now then, captain calling. When I give you the word I want you all to jump up and down.
Stewardess	Take your belts off and stand up, please.
Captain	One, two, three . . . JUMP!
Sid	They're not going to believe this at work, when I tell them that I jumped all the way to Costa Lotta.
Captain	Captain calling. We're off the ground. I'm proud of you. You can all sit down now.

Dolly	Oh, thank goodness.
Sid	Yes, even these seats feel good after all that jumping.
Stewardess	Now, everybody, we're going to give you lunch.
Dolly	That'll be nice, Sid.
Sid	If the food is like the plane, we'll have to cook it ourselves.
Dolly	Please, miss, how long will it take us to get to Costa Lotta?
Stewardess	One or two hours, madam. Sometimes the captain gets lost when he has to fly over the sea.
Dolly	Oh dear, why does he get lost?
Stewardess	He's only got a road map.
Sid	That's all we need.
Dolly	Oh, look out of the window, Sid. There's a duck flying along close to the plane.
Sid	Yes, and he's flying faster than we are!
Stewardess	Is everything OK, sir?
Sid	Not bad, but tell me, why does our brave captain fly so close to the water?

Stewardess	It's a habit he's got, sir. He likes to be near the sea because he was captain of a ship in the war.
Sid	Thank goodness he wasn't captain of a submarine.
Stewardess	Now, sir, would you like your bag of chips?
Sid	Chips?
Stewardess	Yes, sir. I hope you like them cold.
Dolly	Is that all you've got for lunch?
Stewardess	Yes, madam.
Sid	But the man in the travel shop said there would be all sorts of food. He said we could choose.
Stewardess	That's right, sir. You can choose — you can take it or leave it.
Dolly	Oh, well, two bags of chips then.
Captain	This is the captain here. We're across the sea now. We will be flying overland, going south.
Sid	I hope he's got the map the right way round, or we'll be having two weeks at the North Pole.
Dolly	Here she comes with the chips, Sid.

Stewardess	Here you are, sir.
Sid	Look at this. The chips are as old as this plane. The newspaper round them says Britain has just won World War II!
Captain	Hello, captain calling.
Dolly	Shush, Sid, here's the captain.
Captain	You may have seen that this plane had four engines when we were at the air-port.
Sid	Don't tell me someone's pinched one of them.
Stewardess	Just listen to what the captain has to say, sir.
Captain	Don't panic, but one of the engines has stopped working. We're now flying on three engines. This means we can't fly as fast, so we'll be about half-an-hour late getting into Costa Lotta.
Dolly	Oh, what a pity. Still, half-an-hour late isn't too bad.
Sid	Ah well, back to the chips.
Captain	Hello there, captain calling.
Sid	Look out, here he is again.

Captain	I'm sorry to have to tell you, but one of the other engines has now stopped working.
Sid	I think this plane is on strike.
Captain	This means that we're now flying on two engines. So we'll be about one hour late getting into Costa Lotta.
Dolly	I hope the food's good at the hotel, Sid. What do you think we'll have for dinner tonight?
Sid	Custard and kippers.
Dolly	Don't be silly, Sid.
Sid	I'm not being silly. The food's very funny out there, very funny. It's all frogs' legs and sheep's eyes. It doesn't lie there on the plate like British food. It hops around and winks at you.
Dolly	As long as I can have a nice cup of tea, I don't mind what it does.
Sid	But they don't make tea out there like they do at home.
Dolly	Don't they?
Sid	No, out there they fry it.
Captain	Ummm... captain calling.

Sid	Oh no, what is it this time?
Captain	I'm sorry to have to tell you, but another engine has stopped. This means we'll have to fly very, very slowly. We'll be about two hours late getting into Costa Lotta.
Sid	This is the limit. First, one engine goes so we're half-an-hour late. Then another engine goes and we're one hour late. Then another engine goes and we're stuck in this plane for two hours more. There's only one engine left!
Dolly	I hope that one doesn't stop or we'll be up here all day.

The Island

4 parts:
Sid, Dolly, Captain, Kong

Sid	Well, this is a big mess.
Dolly	Now, don't get upset, Sid.
Captain	Yes, cool down. Pull yourself together.
Sid	Pull myself together? I'd like to pull you apart!
Captain	But why blame me?
Sid	Well, you were flying the plane, weren't you?
Captain	Yes.
Sid	And you came and told us that the engines had stopped working.
Dolly	So you put the only parachute on.
Sid	And we held on to your legs.
Captain	Well, there you are. I saved your life.
Sid	Yes, but then comes the nasty bit.
Dolly	Yes, Sid's right.

Sid	You, me and Dolly jumped. But then what happened? All the engines suddenly started to work again!
Captain	Well, how was I to know?
Dolly	And then the plane went off without us!
Captain	Well, I couldn't chase it, could I?
Dolly	And everybody else was still on the plane.
Sid	So the others have all gone to Costa Lotta.
Dolly	And we've landed on this rotten little island.
Sid	Yes, look at this place. It's just a heap of sand and rock with a few trees.
Captain	And that pink monkey.
Sid	As I was saying. It's just a heap of sand and rock with some trees and a pink monkey.
Kong	I'm not a monkey. I'm a gorilla.
Sid	Oh, I beg your pardon. So here we are. There's just you, me, him, and King Kong.

Dolly	Sid, that monkey spoke!
Sid	Yes it did! You're right!
Dolly	Sid, I don't like the look of it. That gorilla looks a bit ... um ....
Captain	Pink?
Dolly	Yes, it looks a bit pink and big and hungry.
Sid	OK, what do you think we should do?
Captain	Well, let's not panic. Just play it cool. Take it easy.
Sid	OK.
Captain	Then run!!
Sid	Right. Let's go. Come on, Dolly!
Kong	Here, hang on! Wait for me!
Captain	He's coming after us. Keep going. Run round the island.
Dolly	Don't eat me! Don't eat me!
Kong	I'm not that hungry.
Sid	You know, there's something funny about all this. If you're a gorilla how is it you can talk?
Dolly	I've never seen a gorilla talk before.

Kong	Of course gorillas can't talk. Don't you know me? Don't you know who I am?
Dolly	I don't think so. I think I would remember if I had met you. I don't know a lot of pink gorillas.
Kong	You have met me before. It's me!
Sid	Who is 'me'?
Kong	Don't you remember? 'Hands up, this is a stick-up'? Banks Travel?
Dolly	Oh, Sid, it's him. It's the bank-robber.
Sid	Oh, it's Harry!
Kong	Yes, don't you remember? That chap gave me a holiday in Costa Lotta.
Dolly	Oh yes, that's right, he did.
Sid	Well, pardon me for asking, but if you got a holiday in Costa Lotta, what are you doing here? Why are you dressed as a pink gorilla?
Kong	I'm under cover. This is my hide-out.
Captain	Why do you need a hide-out?
Kong	The cops are after me.
Captain	Why are the cops after you?

Kong	I had a go at robbing the bank at Costa Lotta.
Sid	What!? Why did you try to rob the bank at Costa Lotta?
Kong	Well, I like to think big. I stole a calendar one time and all I got was twelve months. So now I go for the big stuff, like banks.
Sid	So what did you do at Costa Lotta?
Kong	Well, I had this great plan. There are always some cops at the door of the bank. So I got this gorilla outfit. It was a good way to get past the cops.
Captain	Why was it a good way to get past the cops?
Kong	Well, have you ever seen a pink gorilla rob a bank?
Dolly	No.
Kong	Well, there you are then. A fool-proof plan. They'd never suspect!
Sid	So did it work?
Kong	Yes and no.
Captain	Come on then. Tell us about it.
Kong	Well, they spotted me right away. I

	never got past the door. They knew what I was up to.
Dolly	Well, it was a bit of a funny plan, Harry.
Sid	Yes, it was a good try. But don't you think you stuck out a bit, dressed as a pink gorilla? That outfit doesn't help you to blend in!
Kong	Oh, I don't think it was the outfit that gave me away.
Dolly	What was it then, Harry?
Kong	I think it was the stocking over my head and the shot-gun.
Sid	Oh, no!
Captain	So how did you get away?
Kong	Well, I shot off down the road to the sea. I saw this little speed-boat by the beach. So I jumped into it and here I am.
Captain	So where are the cops?
Kong	I was too fast for them. It was just a little speed-boat. But it was fast.
Sid	But they'll still be out looking for you. They'll spot you if they pass the island.

Kong	No they won't. They'll never spot me. I took the stocking-mask off and dumped the shot-gun.
Sid	That's good thinking. That's very smart.
Captain	Wait a minute. Did you say 'boat'?
Kong	I think so.
Captain	Great! A boat! We can smash it up and use the wood to make a raft. Then we can get away from here.
Sid	Now why didn't I think of that?
Dolly	Let's get the boat. I want to get to Costa Lotta.
Captain	Where is the boat?
Kong	I put the rope round a pole that was stuck in the sand. It's here somewhere. You can't miss it. It's a big pole with a sign on that says 'Danger – Gorilla'.
Captain	Let's all split up and try to find it.
Sid	OK. Dolly and I will go this way. You and he can go that way.
Captain	OK. We'll give you a shout if we find it. Off we go.
Dolly	There it is. There's the boat.

Sid	Great. I'll just give a shout.
Dolly	There's no need, Sid. There's Harry right behind you.
Sid	Oh! You made me jump, Harry. I didn't see you standing there.
Dolly	We found the boat, Harry.
Sid	So let's get the captain and get away.
Dolly	I don't think he can hear you, Sid. Say it again.
Sid	Harry, we've found the boat. Look, here's the boat.
Dolly	What's up with him, Sid? He just grunts. Maybe he still can't hear you. Try again.
Sid	It must be that outfit. He can't hear so well if he has that gorilla mask stuck over his head.
Dolly	Try and shout into the mask.
Sid	OK. Here goes. HARRY! HELLO, HARRY! WE'VE GOT THE BOAT!! OK?
Dolly	Oh, Sid. I think you've upset him. What's he doing?

Sid   Harry! Harry! I don't like this. Put me down! I don't like it up here. AAAAAAGH!!

Dolly   You know, Sid, there's something funny about Harry.

Sid   Oh, yes, very funny. Ha! Ha! AAAAGH! Harry, don't swing me round like that. Put me down!

Dolly   Last time we saw Harry he was pink. Now he's gone brown.

Sid   And I think I'm going green. Harry! Stop throwing me up in the air. I don't feel very well.

Dolly   Sid, I don't think that's Harry at all. I think that's a real gorilla!

Sid   Oh no. AAAGH!!!

   [S–P–L–A–S–H]

Sid   He threw me in the water!

Dolly   Come on, Sid, run! Don't let him catch you!

Sid   I'm coming, Dolly. Help! I'm coming!

Dolly   Let's try and find the captain, and the real Harry.

Captain	We're over here.
Kong	Come on, behind this rock.
Sid	Oh, thank goodness we found you. There's a real gorilla over this side of the island.
Captain	So you think you've got problems? We've just seen a boat full of cops land on the other side of the island. They're on the beach.
Sid	That's not our problem. That's Harry's problem. The cops are after him, not us.
Dolly	Don't be so mean, Sid. Harry is our friend. We've got to help him.
Captain	We'd better get that speed-boat and get going.
Kong	I don't think so.
Captain	Why not?
Kong	Well, first of all I can see that gorilla sitting in it. And the other thing is that there's no petrol left in it.
Dolly	Oh dear, what are we going to do?
Captain	I've got an idea.
Dolly	Tell us your plan.

Captain	Well, if Harry runs on to the beach the cops will see him.
Sid	I think we can bet on that.
Captain	So then he runs off round the island.
Kong	But the cops will come after me!
Captain	That's it. They go after you. Then we run down to the beach and nick their boat. Then we can get away.
Dolly	But what about Harry?
Kong	Yes, what about me? How do I get away?
Captain	You run off round the island, OK? And you keep on running till you've gone all the way round. It's not so big, it won't take long.
Kong	I get it! So I go right round the island and come back to the cop's boat.
Captain	That's it.
Sid	Then Harry jumps in and we're away.
Kong	That's a great plan. So we leave the cops stuck on the island.
Sid	With the real gorilla!

Captain	Let's get on with it. Off you go, Harry. Get out there and make the cops run after you.
Kong	Right. Here goes. Hey, cops, come and get me! Yoohoo! Last one to the beach is a silly kipper!
Dolly	There he goes.
Captain	And there go the cops. Let's get across to the boat!
Sid	Jump in!
Dolly	Give me a hand.
Captain	I'll get it started.
Dolly	Here's Harry!
Sid	Goodness, that was fast. He can shift when he has to.
Captain	Jump in, Harry. That's it. OK, hang on, here we go!
Dolly	We're away. Costa Lotta, here we come.
Sid	Ha, ha! You left the cops standing, Harry.
Captain	Yes, ha, ha, ha, they're left stuck on the island.

Sid	Yes, ha, ha, ha, ha. The funny thing is that I bet they think the other gorilla is you, Harry. Don't you think that's funny!?
Captain	Yes, Harry, can you see them trying to pull the gorilla mask off a real gorilla?
Sid	Come on, Harry, that's funny isn't it?
Captain	Come on, Harry, have a giggle!
Sid	What's the matter, Harry, don't you think it's funny?
Dolly	Sid, I think something's up.
Sid	What do you mean, Dolly?
Dolly	Look. Harry's gone brown again.